Dead Flowers.

Independently written.

ISBN: 978-1-79480-808-9

Enjoy.

Dead Flowers

By: Oliver Amatist

This book is dedicated to Brendan David Hauer, and family.

Based on a true story.

Turn of the Sun

The sun just rose in lost connections.
Please undo the times we have held onto believe,
In false hope, dreams, and expectations.

I'm just glad those two came out alive.
In due time,
It's overwhelming inside.

Chapter One

Taking the High Road

"Look into his eyes, son...

Look into his eyes and say it!

Look into his eyes, son!

Look into his eyes and say it!!"

Within a blink.

Within a mere glimpse of the other side,

I realized.

This man does not own me.

I am free to leave at any time I please.

This day is here to show me,

Within a blink is what this memory will be.

I stare at blanks.

Uncovered army men and tanks.

Cap guns in a children's war.

Synonymous to the momentum of memory.

In real time, I am understanding,

What I refused to accept as a child,
Will follow me,
Because freedom hasn't become what it will be.

"Look into his eyes son!
Look into his eyes and say it!"
The echo of intuition attacks with precision,
The voices I hear are listening,
I scream, "Fuck it!"

Better late than never.
I bet it's time I got wet
And paint a picture in the sand,
I'll paint a picture for this old man,
But I won't stand to be degraded.
I won't stay where I am hated,
I won't play the game of blaming,

Despite the residue of shame,
Coming with this house and my name,
Like magic, I can't walk away from this.
There's too much here.

Too many holes in the walls.

Lord knows I know how they got there.

Here I sit. Stand.

And laugh at hell.

Thinking, "What a perfect reflection he sees of himself."

I yell,

"You call me the *sinner*, but your face exclaims shame,

You are hiding from the fact that you erase time with atrocity.

All you want is *control*.

You want me to shut up so you can speak.

Well, here's what I think."

And there was silence.

Left with two options.

I can stay and speak with the police,

Or I can leave,

With the shirt on my back,

Sixty bucks and some weed.

Without a doubt in my mind,

With a hint of arrogant confidence,

I head East, up hills and down streets I roamed as a child.

It couldn't have been much more than a mile.

When three lights changed,

And I watched my shadow cross the street.

With a chokehold's breath,

I intersect with a statue's suggestion.

Mother Mary points in the direction

Dictating the path of my existence.

Coursing through the veins in my ears,

Are words breaking the blood brain barrier,

"GO HOME, my son.

Give up before the world.

Just. Go. Home..."

Reluctance ensues,

"NO!

I WON'T!

I don’t need another.

Reason to hate.

No more white lies deemed to create a false sense,

Of what this has become.”

Between the focus of two lines.

Resides a memory that refuses to be blocked.

It’s safe to say since I was eleven,

I was in shock.

The crossing gates relay a wicked wreckage

That sends a message to my brain.

This is where Brendan stays,

Six feet deep in his grave.

I point at the ground, breakdown, and pray.

Because unlike him,

I do not know where I will stay tonight.

Sitting, glued.

Stuck to the image of him in his youth,

The tombstone blues,
I rip the grass straight from its roots.
And through all this emotion,
All of this trauma,
I ponder the concept of Nirvana,
And how to conjure the dead.

Within the grooves I place a single amethyst crystal.
"To ward off the negative energy," I think to myself.
But I am pulled through the roots,
A subliminal vortex rips me through
A Catholic presentation,
Of death and dictation.

Hail Mary,
Full of grace,
Your shadow covers Brendan's face.
The day his brain was shaved from oxygen,
The day he disappeared in grace.
Crossing planes of reality,

To the underground, I proudly embark,

To uncover a genocide of mind and parking fees.
A consciousness unknown to the common thief,
A place beneath the city,

Where the humans are plenty.

There isn't a place that wouldn't serve you,
Flesh makes flesh deserve you.
And they feast.
Tomatoes are kief,
Kief is made of you and me.
Humans separated in the vortex of a soul chamber.
Switching places-in reality.

This is just a thought in my mind,
As I leave the cemetery.
Defined.
Contributed,
As a patron,
If you will,
Where the dead lie still.

Penetrating the waves that communicate and spill out into the streets,

Where I walk,

Continuing East.

"To home," I think.

---

22 degrees. Sunny.

Idiots freeze, I find it funny.

Be a meathead,

Be an inbred,

You know what they said yall,

We're all just inbred.

We set out for fire escapes.

Running from torture, running with blades.

Our frowning faces never complain.

Running from heaven,

We're all insane.

The persistent beating of the city

Makes strolls down the street more of a slide,

Often-times reuniting the mind.

As the night becomes apparent.

I search for my friends down in Mountlake Terrace.

Where clowns run the streets,

And the cameras never click.

So, I flick this cig and it lands on a leaf.

It burns to the ground and spins my beliefs,

30 degrees separates him from me.

Cut.

From the second hand of sympathy.

I got nine lives and a bottle of whiskey.

Holdin' onto the week.

I bet he knows that she misses me.

Fuck it.

I just can't sleep.

Up all night roaming the streets,

An idea renders me into a spectrum of risk,

Where possession and value diminish

In the eye of a runaway kid.

“Hey, Eddie?” [It’s almost 4:20 A.M.]

He answers, “What’s up?”

“I got my dad’s car, we’re going to Oregon.”

“When?”

“Right now.”

One technicality away from grand theft auto,

I couldn’t find a place to sleep, so you know my motto

Peddle to the metal, I must admit,

This sixty bucks would be a lot better in liquid.

Flooring it down I-5,

I look Eddie in his eye,

And lay it down.

“Hey, Eddie?

Do you believe in magic?

The spark that bleeds beneath each match stick?

The havoc?

The tragic?”

Pushing eighty down an empty freeway,

I come to grips with the words I am about to say.

Less the 24 hours away from the missing persons list.

I say hey,

"Load a bowl and put some of this on it."

I hand him a bag smelling of plastic and death.

The real reasons that kids can't save the world if they are kept,

Institutionalized from K to 12.

This here, is dreams,

And, "We are escaping hell."

Somewhere between 90 mph and one-twenty,

I realized something *pretty* damn interesting.

We would arrive in Portland,

The dreamy city,

Around sunrise.

The goal is to hold it in,

As long as you can.

But man, if I followed the rules

We'd be in a ditch somewhere around Dike Access Road,

I tell him, “Just a little bit.”

And I smoke that shit.

Along with my last roach clip.

At this point I’m neither alive, nor dead.

Stuck in a sequence between lines and pavement.

I’m not swerving,

I just needed to make a statement.

So, I inhale.

One breath in.

One breath out.

One eye dilates.

One eye shouts,

“Look into his eyes, son!

Look into his eyes and say it!”

It rings around my head as I swerve back onto the pavement.

And before it’s too late,

Eddie looks me in the eyes and states,

“Maybe, I should drive...”

The drive back was alright.

Stuck in morning traffic on I-5.

We split a tab in half.

"To see if it's real," I tell Eddie.

But in all reality.

I wasn't ready.

I wasn't ready for what was about to come.

In my head, under the sun.

This is where the graveyard replicated a gun to my head.

I can head home and tell my dad where I've been.

But it was more than that.

To the naked eye we had a family life.

We loved each other and cared for ourselves.

We talked about nothing.

Communication wasn't even a thing.

To head home and tell my dad where I've been

Was to shoot myself and remember why I left.

Abuse has no words in the silence of night,

When no one can see or hear you,

No one can try to stop the breathing.

I'm pumping gas at 9 in the morning.

Practicing what I'm going to say to my dad.

The pump ever expanding and contracting in my hand.

When I walk up those steps

I won't see a home.

I'll see the decomposition of divorce,

The direct impact of the force of trauma,

Memories of why I wasn't saved by my mama.

I'll hear radio reports to local police,

Ultimately defining our dysfunction as a domestic disturbance.

I'll see a coat closet filled with fleece and the scent of something piercing.

I'll be screaming for justice.

Not merely a "Suspicious Circumstance."

"Where the FUCK have you been?" My dad says,

"I almost reported the car stolen and now

I'm late for my vacation."

"You don't want to know what's going through my head."

I said, with that hint of arrogant confidence.

So, I left.

Again.

Because I would rather be on the streets than stuck,

Agoraphobic, with the memories of a horrific childhood experience,

Repeating in my head,

Every day, when I wake up.

I had enough.

The Path of Least Resistance

This here, in my hands, is nothing more than an hour glass.
Time paves each grain of sand and marks the hours pass.
As each grain stumbles through a maze of consciousness,
We begin to identify ourselves with the others.

This is my faction and my temple.
It exemplifies my drollery.
In all reality I cannot see the revelations forthcoming.
As I make my way through a labyrinth of integrity,
Wondering,
Will the next grain be brilliant?
Am I worthy of serenity?

I have reached the culminating point of hierarchy.
My temple is my paradigm.
My body is my guardian.
My path is one in which I choose,
The aftermath I cannot lose.

I have reached the ambit.

My prior is clear.

The maze in which I reside will return to me with fear.

Fear of predicaments and botheration.

Fear of a wasteful trace I left to hinder.

But as I rise above and follow a path of least resistance.

I will experiment with methods and persistence.

I will come to know myself and others.

Through an objective perspective a mirror cannot surrender.

When I look into a mirror, does it appear to reflect,

The parts of me I so frequently forget?

From the right angle I can see,

The lack of trust I have in me.

Chapter Two

Finding a Place to Sleep

Time and time again,
I see reflections of a frozen mirror image.
Let's retrace our steps,
To see what it takes to make angels reflect
That we are one in the same,
Blessed rose peddle dreams,
In sync with an avenue of freedom.
In search of a perfect reflection,

In this dream I can see myself parallel with hell.
I can justify the love we sell.
I am at an apex and I have to ask,
"Is that you, Brendan, that I see through the looking glass?"

Looking back, *at a glance*,
Within a glimpse of the other side,
I realize...

What stops me from falling far behind my past mistakes,

Is my sunny side.
Love and war.
It's love and war.
I cannot wait.

Souls will celebrate the commonly mistaken.
Lost and found beneath willow trees,
Shadows breathe and parallels combine
As we tend to lose sight
Of what is real beyond this whisper in the night,

"I want to go down the slide," I hear in the softest voice.

I blink twice.
Erase my mind and find myself stuck
Between Mother Mary and the big slide.
As if I pointed to the ground and said,
"This is where Brendan died...
And came back to life."

I remember I tried,
To save him,

But he failed to overcome the wrath of monkey in the middle.

All I could do was instruct the other kids to get help.

One ran in the direction of the front office,

One went and got the gym teacher and she performed CPR,

As one kid called 911 from the cell phone he was prohibited to have at recess.

I just held the nerf ball in my hand and prayed.

I thought to myself over and over again,

The simple desperate words,

"Please don't go... Please don't go... Please don't go..."

Brendan was in cardiac arrest,

And half of these kids went on with their recess.

But the stress,

Implemented itself at this moment,

When I had to walk back to class,

As Brendan was rushed to Children's Hospital.

It was probably a solid minute until one child began to cry,

And another,

And another,

And finally, I came to grips with what just happened,

Dead flowers.

Not in the midst of my peripheral focus,

But right in front of me.

And to my left,

And to my right.

Dead flowers circulating through my mind.

Dead flowers I find all the time.

These dead flowers shine my mind back into lucidity.

Again.

I head East.

Down streets I roamed as a child.

Wondering the true meaning of divine compare.

I wander into the graveyard where smiles can share the experience of tears.

I think,

"You didn't know him like I did."

In a conversation that appears to be with myself,

A near recital of words,

"I spent years by his side... He couldn't walk or talk...

Man, he couldn't even go down the big slide.

But I remember the day,

His heart caved outward and he smiled through the phone and said,

'I love you, Matthew'"

But this time I can't stop and say hello,

I'm just looking for direction.

Just trying to find a place to sleep and avoid the oncoming snow.

I head to where the 206 meets the 425.

With the understanding that this might be the rest of my life.

From couch to couch,

I'll drift away before I die.

But it's like the forces of nature want to distract me.

A palindrome of consciousness like nicotine I breathe,

I head East down streets I roam as a teen.

And the hardest part about sudden homelessness strikes me.

Winter is coming and I'm spending half my nights covered under trees,

While the other days I sneak into vacant houses for shelter.

Dipping out before someone can notice.

The rest is a constant battle.

Every day I must decide.

Do I sleep or eat tonight?

Do I cry or see the light?

My plight is not even half as hard as the average homeless life,

And the biggest difference is that I can go back to what my father calls, "Home."

But that would mean having my dignity stripped,

Privacy diminished,

Verbal and physical punishment

Over dishes left dirty in the basement.

But hold up,

Don't open the fridge.

It's filled with blood and guts.

You see this is where humans make lust.

Where hate has a certain touch.

Where dogs went missing and the holes in walls

Tell a story of seven 9-1-1 calls.

In the end, who has the deed?

When police report a domestic disturbance.

It's the only thing they can see.

But that is no longer me.

As I walk over to Eddie's

I nonchalantly remember horrific entropy entities.

And put them in their past.

Because tonight I will sneak into a friend's house,

Through the window when his parents are asleep.

Tonight, I can sleep.

Tomorrow, I can eat.

Kombucha and Ketamine.

Slick as the sleeves on interdimensional leaves.

Ecstasy sees.

Heaven isn't spent on dimes.

It's spent on weed.

Existential breeze captures me.

Nirvana barks.

I am dark when I embark on the light of my love whom will always spark forgiveness.

The mushrooms tell a story of mountains and molehills.

Somewhere in between getting murdered and becoming famous.

When I thought my hair was worms, my thoughts were dangerous.

Heavin forbid we become what we mention.

When we are ever so slightly held in a palindrome of direction.

Stuck in cells.

Recess bells.

Mother Mary yells

"What a perfect reflection we see of ourselves."

I see faces, not the clothes.

Ice cold isles that line the rose-

Garden, where we have spent,

Too many days sitting on the bench.

In due time, we all find-

-Here, let's pick 'em.

Me and Eddie stand still.

In front of a batch of mushrooms,

"They look just like them," I say to myself.

This is why my health is on the streets.

Because come ups like these never seem to be real.

Desperately strung out on thousands of mics,

Months on end,

I decide to myself, "This must be them."

But I'm in no condition.

You see, the mushrooms are you friends

When you're homeless they mean rent.

But no one checked the head.

They were Amanita's instead.

You see, I ate them first.

But I was too spun out on L,

I should have never trusted myself.

I was lucky I didn't die.

When three weeks rolls by and everyone complained,

I found myself dead eye in range with a deranged Oxycontin addict,

Who decided my brain is better spilt down the steps.

I fought for my life and in moments I blead.

What would you do with a .22 pointed at your head?

Mushrooms meant rent, but this wasn't his game,

He made it clear there was a hit on my head.

So, I left,

Broken phone, broken skull, broken tone.

I blead, down the streets, before I went home.

What a miraculous return it was.

I never thought I would spend my 18th birthday in the hospital,

Or my 25th

Or my 11th

You see, after Brendan nearly passed,

I spent years waiting for him in every class,

The day he went into cardiac arrest,

Was the day I stopped eating.

I would sit patiently waiting through the lunch period,

And eventually the school became concerned.

So, they brought in a therapist,

To help me “process.”

They had me stay in for recess,

The teacher’s had a buffet,

And they just wanted to say,

“You can have some.”

But in my mind, it was as if to say,

“Brendan’s not here, let’s have a buffet!”

And I cried.

Tears ran down through my skeletal pride,

And angel's defeated demons as they arose,

From a broken rose on recess paint.

This is the day I declared Brendan a saint.

A martyr if you will.

Death painted across the playground was the projection of the youth's bad will-

Still, I couldn't fathom what was about to be.

My head was craving,

A surge through my occipital lobe,

Now that we are both twelve years old.

My first visit to the ICU at Children's Hospital,

Was kind of awkward.

I thought he would be awake,

And we could talk,

I could show him the medal I won.

I definitely thought he would be able to walk,

But it turns out,

We couldn't even see him.

He was in no condition.

"Brendan's hooked up to a lot of machines,"
They said to me.

As stories fade and integrate,
A fellow mate of mine,
Who spent the days and nights,
Inside and out with me.
Contemplates life back out on the streets.
As I lived with temporary amnesia,
From a blow to the head,
He spent the fall with me,
But in winter he left.
His name was Anthony,
And I haven't seen him since,
The day he ran away,
With all of my cents.
But I'll always remember him.
As a runaway kid,
Who was beaten by the system.

Who had a brain in his head,

But Uncle Sam has plans to build

A pipeline from youth to jail.

And this was a truth,

As bold as making bail.

“I love you Anthony,”

I say to myself.

It wasn’t like I wanted to leave, I needed to.

Survival means that certain things go unsaid,

Survival tries to itemize the contents of your soul,

The contents of my head, projects.

I fear the words circulating through my head.

So, I left,

Behind me an upside down house filled with memories

Of being whipped with a belt,

Screaming and screaming,

I know that what I felt when I was there, was fear.

I lived in fear of being myself.

I lived in fear of the man who tells me he is my father,

I lived with too much respect.

But what I didn't have, was a stable nest to retreat to,

Oregon, was like the wild west,

And Greg, was a friend who never checked to see if I

Was all right,

But he gave me some of the best blotter these kids had ever tried.

And I began to make a name for myself,

With a piece of Oregon pride.

My birth certificate says a lot about me,

Born in Emanuel Hospital, Portland, Oregon,

11:11 A.M. on October 28th, 1992.

But when I did a FOIA request,

They said, "We have no records of you,"

But that is beside the point.

Vagabond Ballad

Come with me and explore the danger and the trust.
With vagabonds and coffee cups we talk of life's greatest crutch.
We twine the alibi to align in perfect direction.
Within your mind lies the eye's version of perception.

At night he sighs of compromise from the factors and traits.
Born again this dividend is more than love and hate.
"Eye spy with my eye an oncoming train!" He said.
Hitch a ride and drink the shine, made throughout the day.

He was a man with a plan, but never much to say.
To say the least, he hated meat because cows were meant to pray.
For his God and our sun, he had a gun, bullets at his waste.
A nomad soul with tempting tools he used to wicker ways.

Now, on this day, on this train, he hopped and hoped its way,
Led due north where grocery stores would supply his weight,

In smokes and happy folks who shoot the pool and say,

Everything, on their minds, all throughout the day.

Now, this man lived a way we all want to, but never could sustain.

At some point we all sat down and thought of a better way.

To live the lives we once imagined, is to say the dream

Is at least, a common a joke, made of us and our self-esteem.

Now this man stood his own, HONOR read his name.

And on this faithful day, he came to me to say,

"We all have faults, we all have fears, but when it comes to love,

An honest man holds the hand to signify a trust."

So, he grabbed my hand and said to me,

"We share within our valued minds,

The memory of all humankind,

Thus, this moment holds the answer to life's greatest questions.

Do or die, this glass eye, lives within our passion.

There may be times when we cry,

There may be death and debt,

But when it comes to happy homes, you never know what you get."

I ponder this in common time with subtle gestures met,

By the expectations of myself I never will forget.

"But don't get sully, don't get sad," he said to me with motivation,

"Feel free to hate the basic savage ways that thrive in violence."

Now at this point this was his stop.

Home not far away.

He said, "Travel son! The day is young!"

And he went on his way.

With the sun leaking through the pollution of the day

The amber hues and simple clues lead me on my way,

But I never thought my life would take me into modern times,

Where dirt is crime and a sigh at night means a man's okay.

So, I look him up, I call around, looking for a ghost,

Whose shadow roams in the homes made of closet dust.

The elephant epiphany lacks a certain touch.

It seems to me that peace of mind wont amount to much.

But on this day, on this train, with no destination in sight.

I search for a hand to hold all throughout the night.

It seems as if I'm passing by all the moments adding
meaning to this life.

On this train, on this track, without a man in sight.

So, I reach out to grab

Another man without a plan just traveling abroad.

I pull him in. I pull him up

I save a man from becoming train track guts.

He coughs a lot and almost pukes.

He looks at me and says,
"Have I ever met you?"

Now, this one we need not ponder,

Just another man destined to wander.

I said, "Hold my hand and come with me!

Let us manifest our destinies."
He said in response,

"With no God in mind and no money in pocket,
I left it all behind when I chose to hoof it.
I will take your hand with the trust
That you my man have seen enough."

Suddenly, I realize the energy is real,
Everyone I've ever loved his here riding these wheels.
On this train that runs on brains
With all thoughts concealed.

For with this man, I share with him a meal.
Made of trust.
Made of duck. Made of fish at sea.
I think, "In a way we are thieves, riding to the sea."

Now, no one knows what happened next.
No one knows if someone tied their wrists,
To the train that runs on brains
Of common Christmas kids.

So, this kid will push this train,

Pretending life is just a game,

Never knowing the decade to come

Could withhold a vagabond

Holding hands with people on the street.

Instead, he will think of better ways to feed the meat to common folks

Made like you and me,

Who live in homes, with shiny cars, and all the finest meats.

But between you and me.

Frequently, I think.

I would rather be hopping trains.

I would rather be on the street.

Chapter Three

Getting There

Lids slowing pushing down.
Peripherals disarmed.
My retina dissolves color of charm.
I open my eyes and engage in the star.

The morning light piercing my eyes.
Street sides flip inside my mind.
Passing through the occipital side.
It slides right through the memory,
Or lack there of
The echoing in between the scene in my head,
An awaking,
Undead.

Too much color dispensed in my brain.
I'm crunching on sidewalks and learning the names
Paved in the pavement, where I sit on this day,
Frying on acid, loving the wave.

My lids stick and shivers my wrist,
I can't remember what last night did.
But this, clearly written in the pavement,
Two lovers of notice, making their statement.

Click.
What is best, is not what is given to me.
So, I sit back and rest
I'll sleep through the day,
I bet it won't stay this bright.
I'll sleep on my other side.
"Goodnight."

I pretend to pull the covers over my torso.
On the sidewalk I remain,
Sleeping through a memory with fangs.
If you die in your dreams,
You die in the day,
Or so they say.

One eye crusted and fucked.
One eye opens up.

Slick to the wrist I'm tied to the door of this Lincoln.
And I'm just a kid, 8 or 9, just thinking,
How do I escape this feeling?

I pull on the door handle, but it had nothing to give
As spiders appear at the top of my head.
Jumanji in size and growing in numbers.
Drool from the fangs of these salty purveyors.

The hair on my arm, static and prompt.
Tied to the webs are every stressful thought.
Descending on vines, I heard what you said,
"When I am asleep, I am not in my head."

I scream for help, the car driving itself.
It punctures the star like a solar flare.
I'm screaming for help,
But no one is there.

I am scared straight, I scream and awaken
Back on the sidewalk with narcoleptic precision.
It's almost as if I am traveling dimensions,

Until I lose my circadian rhythm,

And that's the precision of sleep on the streets,
When there's no catcher to filter your dreams.
It carries on through dusk and through dawn,
And on throughout the day.

I decide to leave Seattle behind,
With tricks up my sleeve,
I'm heading South,
To brighten the streets.

"Portland is home," I say to myself.
There's a process in play,
And I am gripping with stealth,
Greg tells me, "I wouldn't do this for anyone else."

The blotter is perfect.
I'm drifting away from everything held behind the curtain.
Cities away from being a drone.
I'm calling it quits and heading home.

I am nothing more, or less then the feeling
Of a dream soaking my iris.
The sun is all I can see.
When I close my eyes there are spots in disguise.
Made of symmetry between the leaves and the sky,
The light is alive.
On this last ride down the Washington coast.
When you lose your mind,
You lose your home.

Wishing I was stoned, I conquer the phantom torso.
"All I need is a place to sleep,
And you would be my hero."

---

3 hours had passed and alas!
We made it.
A city made of wet cement statements.
A new era of time and dictation.
Found on the walls are aesthetic religions.
I read the words sprayed on the stone,
"The kid's want acid."

I laugh,

And pretend I don’t have anything in my hand,

But something is telling me I’m not far from them.

We head to East Portland,

Up and down streets I lived in when I was just 2.

Pictures of us on the Eastside, by Burger Country,

Where my dad would make the eats.

I can remember this in my dreams,

Creating a cryptic sensation of truly being in a heaven of home.

No bedroom means no war zone.

I stop by my buddies, just to charge my phone.

But it was too early for him.

I was a kink in the chain.

I remember Greg asked, “What’s your last name?”

“Dragovich,” I said.

“Sounds Russian, you’ll be fine.”

And before I could ask him why, he dipped.

Leaving me stranded just off South East Division Street

With just a quarter sheet.

Tiny soaked doves in my pocket.

I render myself useless in the East

"Back to the Westside,' I think.

After all it's just a bus ride away,

Down the way,

Past Burnside.

When I arrive is where I am provided,

A couch to rest my sun soaked iris.

Combining the features of day and night

I open the door to find Bob and Skylar.

Two drifters I met in the actual hour of defeat,

Because picking up sheets is more than a job,

It's a duty.

To serve and protect the freedom of expression.

I hold close to my heart a piece of the immaculate precision.

The amethyst rock distilled in his grave.

Here I hold its counterpart and say, "I'm back from Seattle."

"Welcome back mate," I hear the trap house say.
And again, the words repeat in my head,
"Look into his eyes, son.
Look into his eyes and say it."

But I would rather look him in the eyes after I made it.
The strip club capital will say it for me.
With dollars and bars I look to stars and think,
This couch is more like home, and less like the street.

The trap house sees me.
It's breathing.
My eyes dilating and twitching.
The vortex of this building truly traps your soul.

The owner from Oakland is a pimp by trade
And the drifters, like me, are supposed to sleep in the basement.
I didn't know, too tired to show my gratitude.
I leave my L on the table and fall asleep on the couch.
As I rest my eyes and wait for another day.

Rise and shine and give God your glory, glory!
The true meaning hides behind laws of the land.
I open my eyes to a conversation, so stunning,
Living on the streets is illegal, or something.

To say the least, I'm happy I have a place to brush my teeth,
But some sort of jabbering awakens me.
"He's been asleep here all night and we don't know who he is,"
Someone says as my eyes slowly shift.
"I know him, by Cosmic," says Bob with courtesy of hardship.
"He needs to talk to Minion," a prostitute's opinion.

Here I am, waking up,
Stuck to the last few months,
I was in and out of my Dad's place for a couple years
And he finally had enough.
He bribed me with $2000.00 to not press charges,
Kicked me out and said, "Good luck!"
Which, in itself, is fucked.

I didn't have enough time to find a place to live,

Let alone work,

So here I am, in a trap house in Tigard, Oregon,

Wondering if this pimp from Oakland can provide a home,

For a disabled drifter.

I just wish my dollars wouldn't wither.

I wish I had my cat with me.

She reminds me of Brendan, for some reason,

I wish...

I could remember my first kiss.

Instead,

I remember a phone call I would never forget again.

It went something like this,

"Is Brendan home?" I politely ask Mrs. Hauer,

"Tomorrow is my birthday, and I was hoping we could do something together."

I hear some screams in the background and Mrs. Hauer replies,

"He can't talk on the phone tonight." And she hung up.

I screamed at my dad because he was the only one home.

All I wanted was to see my best friend after a summer alone.

I look at the thermostat and it reads: 11:11 PM,

I scream at the top of my lungs, “I wish Brendan was dead!”

And that’s where we left off.

It wasn’t three days later,

The day after my Birthday,

October 29th, 2003,

When Brendan escaped death,

On the playground with, “friends.”

And then...

I started to recall the moments prior.

Epicenter of Soul

From freehand paint, to that stylish hate,
I can see it reciprocate through time and space.
One word, landing on the epicenter of soul.
Until you are told you are too old to speak that childish crack rap.

Who wants to list the exact facts of life?
And tell these kids what a crack pipe is?
Because there's a list of this shit going on during recess
And it's been going on since we were kids.

I've never felt more segregated or demolished,
Diminished or fully polished by the language of skids.
And this influence lands in our heads,
Causing me to need meds.

I think we need a division of harassment feds.
I just lived through eight years of smear the queer,
Denied confirmation to God, because of the words I hear,
Uttered from the mouths of friends,

Can anyone tell me when High School fucking ends?

It's like trying to outsmart stupid with Cupid's mugshot,
Engraved in the language we speak,
Yet somehow, I never heard this when I lived on the street
There is a disconnect between,
Community and Cope,
Home and Dope,
Friends and Foes,
"Fag," and "Bro."

"Bro, look, I don't care what you do in your free time,
Just keep it away from me."
Says a grown man who preached hate speech to humans that bleed relentlessly.
He will see the power of his words when ten years rolls by
And that kid takes the power back.
In fact,
Let him know that I have his back.

When it all boils down to the way we were raised,
Millions of us feel the exact same sensation of pain.

It starts with the word, "fag," and grows into plans to
pepper spray people walking down the Ave.

To raise a nazi flag and demonize the people who stand to
defy it.

It starts with the words we choose to use as children,

It starts with you.

And hear I'm glued to the few who will actually hear these
kids out.

Kids who shed tears from years and years of harassment,

Eventually cratering a hole in the epicenter of their soul,

Let me tell you about when I was ten years old.

Hypertrophic Cardiomyopathy.

A heart condition undeserving on my best friend's body.

A robot heart that shocks the arteries,

When his heartbeat falls out of consistency.

Simply put,

A group of kids called me a fag.

He ran away from the group of kids who supported it.

And this kid could never run away from the defibrillator
inside his chest.

Straight into cardiac arrest,

This kid almost died on the pavement because of the words people said.

I can still see the scar across his chest.

I can still hear the first words he said when he relearned how to speak.

I can still see him in my dreams,

Brendan David Hauer,

RIP.

If you haven't heard from me in a while,

It's because I'm trying to reach self-actualization of speech.

Just trying to teach people what the word, "fag," actually means.

Chapter Four

Merry Pranksters

With all things considered,

I cannot pass,

A bridge that breaks every laugh,

The sap in trees will soothe my wrist

With breaking light as motivation.

Forming the process of photosynthesis.

Cells separate.

Cell can prepare.

Oxygen forming the movement of air.

On deep breath.

One moment.

I'm frozen.

And this is when I realized the power of mindset.

I began to understand that people do things to remind them of when they were young.

And every moment spent in our waking lives is here to test us.

When we fail...

We don't sleep well...
When we sleep well...
We can still fail.
But that is the error of being human,
And when we realize what makes us human,
We will do anything to obtain that.

And this was the moment I knew,
I was a bird in my past life,
Who never learned to fly.
Thrown out the nest by his mother
In a tree just above the property where I would
Live lives over and over again,
In the den, with crystals on the floor,
Monster trucks and pot plants,
And Dad's devious sweat pants,
He always wears,
When he attacks.
Time warps and wars fought with land mines
In the very yard where I died a dozen times,
Repeat.
Repeat.

Repeat in my head the vacancy fed

To Oxycontin addicts

Right next to my bed.

He doesn't know what he meant when he said,

"I help when I can."

Here I am,

No longer crying,

More or less,

Surviving.

Bob tells me I need to go talk to Minion if I want to stay another night.

I was worried, I didn't have anything in mind of what this conversation

Would turn out to be.

Silently reciting lyrics to a Queen song,

I follow Bob upstairs,

And man did I get an introduction.

Bob's like, "He's fun and somethin',

Chill or whatever."

And Minion simply said,

“Hey man, if you need a place to sleep I gotchu,
I just ask that you take the dog for a walk when you can,
And maybe pay the water bill later down the road.”

And alas!
I fucking feel like I am home.
Just like that drifter said to me back up in Seattle,

But the harsh realities of homelessness still linger upon me.
I need to find a job, as I start this new life.

I head back downstairs to a group of people chatting it up,
Thankfully not about me.

This dude just got out of jail on the Eastside,
He said he was getting shit for having a purple belt,
And I said, “Hey, well, I need a belt.”
And he graciously gave it to me.

Bob tells him, “He just got back to Portland.”
“Welcome home kid,” and he gave me the gift.
And my lids are slowly separating.

Defeat was temporary, no longer subsidiary.

This gracious act leaves me with possibility.

Maybe I can find a job and be happy.

Maybe this wasn't a bad decision to spontaneously dip over state lines.

It's fucking cold outside,

And I have a place to sleep tonight,

A sympathetic season breathing deeply through my lungs,

"They call me Cozmic, like kamikaze,

With eyes so wide, he's not blind, but he can't see.

He said, "allow me to show you,

Just how far your fucking mind can take you.

Next step.

Let me take you to the level of this next breath.

Do you believe in magic?

The spark that bleeds beneath each matchstick?

The havoc?

The tragic?

Whether or not you're bound to bleed,

You're bound to see,

Cuz, I know what it's like to take twenty-five hundred mics,

To the dome,

On the daily.

Maybe, your finally ready to step inside your mind and toughen up,

Double up your dosage,

Breathe deep and lose focus,

Sink deep between the sheets,

And own up to the shit you did,

But never noticed.

Don't stop.

Start.

Begin again.

Dismiss the past, or forget to let in,

Messages of love and hate,

Paradigms and riddles played out in fate.

Now.

Stop. Think and Listen.

Take a deep breath and observe the lessons,

Leading you through a journey in life,
A rollercoaster ride,
Hold on tight.

Be the positive to a negative.
Believe it or not,
We can repel the spells that keep people apart.
I am a psychonaut,
Come explore with me,
The seven seas of our minds that combine to spread.
Peace, love, unity, and respect.
Take this time to begin.
Let in and let live.
Take this single moment in time and hit pause.
Stop.
And rewind.
Take this time and release the energy.
Free the beast that you hold so dearly,
Clinging to the back of your tongue.
It's not right.
No.
It's not right.

Take this single moment in time and ride waves guided by the moon.

Laugh as the dollar loses value.

Allow you,

Yourself.

-I got nothin' else,"

I said in a chill battle between some kids in the garage.

With beer pong tables and lots of hours draining away,

Bob and Skylar have been smoking JWH for days.

Pockets filled with powder.

They were getting it on a front from a different pimp.

Bob takes a hit and hints with a devious humor.

"I'm living in one pimp's house and getting JWH from another pimp.
It's fucking double jeopardy."

The trap house begins turning.

Slowly shifting between liquid battles,

There' four people here. Two with vials

Leaving free in a frequency house,

A mouse trap sits on the kitchen floor,

Come closer to the garage and you'll see a trap door,

"If we get raided, you can hide in here,"

Skylar laughed and closed the floor.

I spray him with silly string.

He declares war.

There's a difference between drifting and a homeless décor,

But I'm still eating from dumpsters,

Searching to score.

Not dope, as one might think,

But a job to work,

Peace off the street.

The idealistic community standard lives deep in my psyche,

Running around my own mind, constantly being reminded of Mikey,

And how he left me.

I walk into the basement and Skylar is plotting.

He pours me a full shot of pure LSD, Lavender.

And I start smiling.

"They call me Smiley,"

And I'm happy,

For a *brief* moment.

But the intensity is brighter than a blinding light.

The pimp in this house asked me to stay a night somewhere else,

So, I roll over to the WESNET house,

Where college students and DEA contemplate how,

To truly serve and protect.

This wicked wreckage sends a message to my brain.

I forgot the ergot can make a man go sane.

As bumble bees weave in and out of lanes,

Contradicting the feeling of us all being tamed.

I see, stained,

Odors putrid.

The image of Cupid.

My brain feels stupid.

As a chemical rush surges into my skull.

I most have eaten twenty-fold.

Liquid shin dig,

I end up at my friend’s apartment,

Just down the street.

They said, “Hey man, you can sleep here tonight.”

“Sweet,” I think to myself.

What’s better than friends who don’t pay bills?

Straight trippin’ on L.

I ponder the concept of self.

My own identity,

And what Skylar was truly doing when he poured me that shot.

You see, it wasn’t Bloods or Crips,

It was military and skids.

Undercover kids,

Cops on top of the college game.

“Anything over $200.00 and we turn them in.”

I heard one of them say.

Delusions at bay,

I see...

A leaf...

Falling from thin air.

As the wind flushes its path,

And presses nature against glass.
I start to remember something in my past,
Holding me back,
Retrograde and stacked.
Two arms,
Wait one,
And that rope.
Tied against my throat.
Producing thoughts, like,
“Please just go... Please just go...”

My arm in my throat,
Blacking out from pain,
As red crows circulate,
Above my head.
I bleed out.
In the shower,
Tied together like a severed doll.
The image I see,
Is nothing at all.
Before an FBI surgeon enters and pieces my severed
Arm back together with a pocket laser.

And I wake up.
To my mother,
Screaming at my father.
My leg was broken and I fell on the couch,
And I continued to bleed out.
Police start knocking on the door.
My mom shoved a rag inside of me as my dad
Threatened her life, demanding her to lie,
As the light of my soul starts to die.

I snap out of it.
"I was just five."
I say out loud.

"What was that?" my friend says to me.
"Oh, nothing," I mutter, "Whatchya making?"
"Just some noodles, you poodle,"
And we both chuckle a little bit.

"Yo! Come over and hit this,"
Keith spits from the living room,
"We're making a fort!" of some sort.

And the rest was a complete and total blur.
I passed out on a couch in another person's
House that I have never met.

But at least I am not wet.

Epiphany's Touch

The sun just rose in lost connections.
Please undo the times we have held onto believe,
In false hope, dreams, and expectations.

I'm just glad those two came out alive.
In due time, it's overwhelming inside.
Watch me fall through crescent loops,
Lucidity in the night.

I know it might be hard,
To reach with open arms,
But can you see how hard it is for some kids to breathe?
Maybe we all need something to shock our heart beats.

I know it may seem cold to say just what I see,
But when I think twice and then I, then I speak,
Is when I appear to be,
Merely sequenced to the themes that stream,
Through your beautiful blue carbon eyes.

On second thought, I thought twice.

Chapter Five

Raid Day

Waking halfway up to the words of a military cop;

On a couch with the stain of cigarettes lingering in the air.

I can't breathe and all I hear is,

"He has a family to support in another country."

And immediately my eyes pop open.

"I thought that might get his attention," he mutters.

The stench is something other,

Gasping for air I go to the back porch to smoke,

Just trying to grasp the morning choke.

Trying to avoid-

An evoke of emotion,

Crumbling inside the midst of hail,

Segments of my past seem to prevail,

I have grown stale with this small apartment full of college kids.

The hail picks up as everyone gets prepared for their days,

They say, "You have to leave when we do, but you can come back tonight."

But the trap house hears these words and I am sucked into a lack of light.

My will shrivels.

Anxiety at full scale,

I am pushed into the direction of this pimp,

Who is frankly, in a lot of shit, running a home like he did.

I knock on the door, and Bob lets me in.

“Minion is pissed,” he says.

Fumbling my words, I detour up the cricket steps,

This meant I would have to face,

The disgrace of being homeless once again.

He assures me, “It’s all good, you are my friend,

But I need you to walk the dog every now and then,

And then pick up the water bill before it gets shut off.”

In panic, I agree,

No work means no fancy living,

In a basement with garbage increasing in piles on the side of the house,

I’m like a mouse, trapped in the woodwork.

I mutter, “I need to find work.”

My insides twerk.

Depleting from scratch and win tickets,

And hearing words like, “Molly to the front counter!”

An orange juice will surely fix my mood,

I’m craving moods as I’m smoking Kools,

Wondering if someone knew I was useless.

I can’t seem to find comfort from the prostitute’s purpose,

Malnourished,

I fall asleep on the couch as a party starts its circuits,

Again, in a pimp’s house, that’s more like a circus.

Reverberance and deceit,

I am at least, warm,

But my head space is vacant.

I’m moments away from a damn near panic.

Lightning strikes my mind,

Surface layers begin to shine,

Uninterrupted sleep will always hide,

A soda spilt on the plywood.

“Did he just spill that and walk away?”

I hear someone say as stumble to the bathroom.

“No, I did that, I’ll clean it up,” a woman states.

She wasn’t a prostitute,

But it was hard to tell,

Between vagrants, vagabonds, and liquid L,

Things tend to blend between reality and fantasy,

A hardcore calamity.

When virtue met insanity.

I proudly state, “It wasn’t me!”

But they didn’t care,

In their minds I was a drifter with nothing to share,

And I couldn’t compare this life to anything splendid.

The bathtub was degraded,

By group sex, and bloods in the basement.

One walks up and apologizes to me,

“Sorry bro,”

But I didn’t understand why.

Instead of staying up all night and raging in the vortex,

I pass out on the other living room couch,

And wake up to...

Something simply gross.

"Don't step in dog shit," Bob shakes me awake,

The one responsibility I had was to make sure the dog is OK.

But this liquid shin dig held me closer to fear than aspiration,

And Minion was determined to kick my ass to the curb.

But suddenly everyone retreats to their designated couches,

As military officials walk in, documenting the house with their voices,

Recording.

Recording.

Recording.

"I'm gonna let him go, because I don't know what he has,"

Says a man in full car heart and denim.

I say I'm going to the back porch to smoke,

But in all reality, I dipped out as a military raid was happening inside the house.

I caught a bus to the East side where Love said I could squat until I find a spot to live in.

On my way to the other side I come across two backpacks tied to the bus stop.

It was Christmas day and I assumed these were random gifts given by a thoughtful community member.

So, I rummage through them and take what I need to survive,

But as I am walking away a man comes screaming after me,

“That’s my home MUTHERFUCKER!” he screams.

And I panic.

Not knowing what I am seeing.

As this homeless man starts threatening me,

I drop my bag and say,

“Sorry man! I thought it was abandoned, I just need my phone and sim card back, take the rest!”

And the homeless man achieved robbing me for accidentally robbing him.

I lost 25 sugar cubes with 100 hits of 100 mcg LSD-25 spread out on the cubes.

I think, “Man, now that guy has something to lose.”

And I continue to head East.

Eventually getting a ride from Love, a woman I cherish and love.

I tell her my story and she gave me a replacement vial.

She said, “Fill it halfway with H20 if you want it to be strong,

Fill it all the way up if you need money."

But I forgot to fill it at all.

And I ate three hits of concentrated liquid LSD-25.

And man was I in for a ride.

Head gaskets firing, my head is floating,

Peripherals dying, I'm trying,

To remain calm, as I walk down the sidewalk,

The safe way to Safeway,

Where I enter and see, a pyramid of pop,

Labelled, "Fryday Special."

And I bust out laughing.

The fact that they are mapping out my activities and commercializing my thoughts,

Man, it carried my head right out the store, and back down the sidewalk,

Where I find a Subway gift card on the ground.

My brain is floating,

Heaven is showing me that everybody needs to eat,

There's fifteen bucks on this card, I think, "Neat!"

So, I go to subway.

And eat a sandwich,

With the borderline appearance that I am mentally unstable,

Laughing horrifically at the sandwich,

Like a fable that lost its meaning-in the new age,

Broken bins and heroin dens dictate the precision needed,

Do I go home or dance with the vortex?

Shifting itself in my direction.

Love asks me one simple question,

"Do you want to go with me to Eugene to a house party where you can make some money,

Or do you want a ride back to Seattle?"

Diligently I think,

"I know more people that want this shit up North, I guess it's time to go 'home'."

Icare4myfriend/Instant Messenger I.D.

Living without Brendan at recess led me to ways to voice my trauma in a heartful manner.

I would text people across the country on instant messenger with the tag Icare4myfriend.

I would talk to strangers about how I watched him suffer cardiac arrest and how I wait every day for him to make it home from the hospital.

I grew weary as his mother kept telling me he would be home soon,

But then a year went by and he was still in the ICU at Children's Hospital.

Simply put,

I was in love with him.

Even though he couldn't talk.

Even though he couldn't walk.

I loved him more than anything else.

And I'll never forget the day his mom took us out on a date to see the new Harry Potter movie.

I'll never forget the first words he said over the phone.

I'll never forget him as he is tattooed onto my arm.

I care for my friend,

His smile could heal 1000 words.

Existing for years in a twilight source.

Resurrecting what we feel.

Dear Brendan David Hauer,

"I love you.

This is not the saddest day of my life,

That was the day you died and came back to life,

If you can hear me,

Through the echoes and exclamations defined in the belief

That we are one in the same.

Blessed rose peddle dreams,

In sync with an avenue of freedom.

In search of a perfect reflection.

Because in this dream I can see myself parallel with hell,

I can justify the love I sell,

But above and beyond all else,

I am half a human,

0.5 less than you,

And I would do anything to hear you say,

"I love you, Matthew," over the phone again.

So please,

If you are reading this,

Don't think of me.

Just be.

Happy.

And know.

There is nothing harder than coping with death.

Chapter Six

The Epic Decent

Eye lids crack like broken silence.

Here I ride through rivers and past islands.

Laughing at nothing,

My subway card still had something on it.

I admit,

This is a constant reminder of why justice never lifts,

But Justice is at a rave-stuck in the past,

Justice is her name.

And Justice never lasts,

She only arrives,

Past the broken noises,

Static.

Silence.

I'm just a passenger,

Wondering where my life is.

I panic,

And remember the kids I used to kick it with.

Rocky was her name.

Her hair dyed different every day.

The book she wrote was a façade

And as I shower at a friend's place for the first time in days,

I hit her up and say, "Hey, I've got some liquid, I need a place to stay tonight."

"I'm on my way," Rochell achieves this response with no hesitation.

The breaking beat of my vacation is dwindling my conscious observations,

I'm feeling the force of Oregon and whores,

Riding my back.

My thoughts so loud, I can hear my ears crack,

Ice shackles I'm back in Seattle.

Where money is mandatory,

And the Juggalo's struggle to find this real form of presence.

This liquid dream killer.

Liquid essence.

Perfume, if you will,

Observe the words that make protests stand still,

Rocky yells from her car,

“Hurry the fuck up, I need to get home twenty minutes ago!”

“It’s fucking cold, it might snow, sorry I’m going as fast as I can,”
I tell her with my acid diluting my hand,

So wavy with excursion.

These waves of delusion are perfect,

For someone who has nothing,

But sixty bucks, a vial,

And a need to shave.

We arrive, at her sister’s place.

And the acid is displaced in my brain,

I’m crunching on vibes, just trying to remember names,

She said, “You can sleep here tonight, before we go our separate ways.”

And she hands me a brownie,

She calls it a, “Jefferey.”

I eat it.

Simply because I am hungry.

She starts to confuse me,

Saying I can stay, but I can't,

Simple words her courtesy assures me,

I won't freeze to death on the streets tonight.

But I start to cry,

A simple tear,

A simple Dear, John.

My thoughts so loud, my thoughts are gone,

Like a soldier at war, dealing with divorce,

Combining the reasons we force ourselves to be kind,

She said, "We are going to bed, goodnight."

And I try,

To comfort myself and slide into dreamscape.

But there's a pressure forming on my hand,

I feel the slightest touch of syringe piercing my back-head fringe,

And the piercing feeling digs deeper.

And deeper into my brain.

I wake up as someone slides out the room,

Uncouth.

I hear a child's voice scream inside my head,

"He's dying mom!"

And I tried to go back to bed,
But instead,
I begin to panic,
The poison snake is asleep in the cage,
But the poison is leaking into my brain.
The pain.
Sinister and steep,
Like stairs I'll never defeat.
I try to scream...

Chills over run me,
Was it the snake that bit me?
Was it the Jefferey?
Was it a syringe of heroin meant to kill me in my sleep?
Was it murder?
Or soon to be?
Was it nothing?

My imagination calls 911,
As I am stripped.
Naked and pretending,
This shower will save me.

But the pain is ascending,

A crescendo point of drifting.

I am slowly decaying in my waking body.

Fire fighters and EMTs arrive at the scene.

I tell them there is something stabbing me in the back of my head,

And I fall to the ground,

The firefighter urges me to stay standing,

"What's really happening here?' He asks me.

"IDK, they said I could stay the night and the next thing I know there was a sharp pain in the back of my head," [Like a syringe poking my hippocampus].

"What hospital do you want to go to?" The firefighter asks.

"Swedish, Edmonds."

The EMT takes my shoes and socks off as I am writhing in pain.

He runs a marker gently, diagonally, across my bare foot.

My toes, in reaction, extend outward and apart,

Then they clench tighter than Brendan's heart.

The EMT radios the hospital,
"We are taking him in on basic life support,
Do you know what happened to you!?"

"No."
I respond in tears.

As I am wheeled in, they question my condition.
They put me in a segmented room,
A brain surgeon is in the other room,
And I hear on a walkie talkie,
"POISON CONTROL IS ON ITS WAY!"

They tell me to relax and stay lying down on my side,
The brain surgeon removes something from my brain,
I can feel it slide out of the back of my head,
Like kicking a wall with a toothpick in your toenail,
I feel another syringe injected into the back of my mind,
And slowly, I calm down.
Delusions, derailed.

“Your insurance won’t cover your stay tonight, you need to leave,” A nurse states.

So, within 30 minutes of being wheeled into the hospital on basic life support,

They kick me out and told me I have an hour to get somewhere to sleep before the pain killers kick in.

I think,

“This is the America I live in.”

And each step I take is riddled with despite,

The hunger I had continues to fight my mind,

I’m slipping down sidewalks and opening a chime,

Just wishing my dad will let me stay for the night.

In just thirty minutes I covered enough ground,

To knock on the door at 1 A.M. at my dad’s house,

“What are you doing here?” He opens the door and shouts,

“I just got out of the hospital.”

“No, you didn’t,” he insists.

I hand him the paperwork and the pain killers lead me to the couch,

Where I pass out,

Not knowing what will happen to me in my sleep.

A Simple Song

Your rivers run for miles,
And pave the way for me,
Where I'll awake near the ocean,
With all the time to waste,
All the room to breathe,
And all the space to be at one.

But I haven't seen the sun in months,
Or felt the breeze in this way.
A lack of light that I can't tame.
A lack of light in my day.

Better late than never,
I bet it's time we got wet,
And paint a picture in the sand,
Bury me as we hold hands.

In this critical state.

Chapter Seven

Widowed

A myriad.

Panic buttons and safe locks,

Tick tock my mind goes rick, rock,

The clock clicking in place,

Time is never known,

Because time has no face.

I embrace the person I see,

Running through a concrete meadow,

Something you wouldn't believe.

Brendan rises from his slumber on the black top,

His heart restarts and slowly he stands up.

Arteries as junctions of love,

The anatomy of heart,

Blessed by a dying dove,

I see my love,

Alive and well.

This moment is on repeat-never standing still.

He smiles and waves,

Skipping away,

Back to recess where 5th grade hearts are meant to be.

He blows me a kiss.

I cry tears of joy and awaken from my sleep,

With salty rain accumulating in my teeth.

I scream,

"BRENDAN!"

And I realize it was just a dream.

I slowly begin to piece together my night,

How I ended up back here,

In a house where I was raped,

At the age of seven.

Where I punched seven holes in the walls,

Called the police seven times,

And the countless nights left for me to wonder

Where my mom is and why she left me here.

Divorce storm,

Hording dorms,

Infusion forms,

I have been lured.

Recovery takes patience.

Trust is something I have given but I have not received,

I'm addicted to the drifting ways,

Yet, I can barely sleep.

Nightmares wrench my teeth and plastic guns are buried beneath,

A garden that once was,

Dormant,

Defeat.

I am contemplating schemes,

Ways I can get out on the streets,

Make a living with psychedelics,

Make enough to give someone else food to eat.

Achievement,

Lost in the drift,

It seems as if this is becoming more like a waiting game.

Where all I am allowed is a minimum wage job,

And a degrading mind.

At home:

Constant harassment, day in and day out,

Comments on my pajamas and inappropriate touches,

And who knows what happens when my eyes close,

No one really knows what I am enduring.

No one really knows what it means to live in this house.

The vortex shouts, “COME BACK TO OREGON!”

It falls on a def mind.

Recorded time,

Streamlined existence.

I am trained to take demands and clean up the messes.

And months go by,

With me trying to climb corporate fences.

I was working part time at a Little Ceasar’s.

Just trying to get through school.

My head healed, and the hospital report made me look like a fool,

"Unknown cause of pain," was my diagnosis,
Despite my throat almost closing from swelling.

I remember Love came by, at least it was Jessica,
She offered me a jar of molly,
She said, "Take what you need, we have plenty,"
And I took the smallest, most unique crystal,
And did a bump of K off some dichroic.
And played her a song on my upright piano,
Before she left.
She said,
"You'll get through this."
Or at least that's what I heard.

Months continued to roll by,
Living a traumatized life,
In the same house as my abuser,
Without an option to leave,
Or I would just be on the streets.
And the constant warmth of a house,
Keeps me chained to my beliefs,
So, I look for full time work

Not knowing that my brain is suspended and decaying.
These nightmares and flashbacks are portraying my voice,
To stand up and defend, would give me no choice.

Embroidered on my arm is a cross made with a heart,
Blue as the darkness that never departs.
Like an alien on my sleeve,
Every time I look down,
I am reminded of the first time I saw Brendan,
Out of the hospital.

He was strapped to his wheelchair,
He could hear,
But he couldn't speak,
Crunching a fetal position,
His brain and mind, weak.
But his eyes, so wide, and stunned that he sees,
Me sitting in the front of him,
12 years old,
In disbelief.

I never thought it was this bad.

I thought when he returned home,
Things would go back to normal.
But his road to recovery would take a decade,
And I would eventually lose the memory of his face.

As he uncurls in his chair and blinks twice,
Meaning; yes, yes, I love you too.
I can't help but think,
"I could have done more to save you."
And I think,
"You can do this, I love you."

And I remember hour long phone calls,
Where Brendan would fall asleep,
Just listening to my 12 year old voice over the phone,
Even though he couldn't speak.
But eventually,
Quite eventually,
He muttered the world,
"I love you, Matthew."

And that was the first time I had heard him speak in years.

That was the first time I knew reverberance.

That was the first time I thought, Brendan may never be physically able to play,

But his attitude and heart would always remain in place.

Solar light meets razor sharp eyes.

Depicting the moment between head rest and sunrise.

This hue outlines her intuition,

Burning the vision,

Catastrophic illusions separate a soul from solar,

Bold from bolder-stacked in such a precise way,

The sun rising sets a different day.

The razor sharp ways fuel a wasteful dance,

With lightning bugs holding hands,

And I am left speechless,

As my dad tells me the FBI is looking for me.

Simultaneously, I check my account balance,

And notice $2000.00.

“I’m saved!” I scream and leave a house

With corpses stuffed in the foundation,

Body parts in the fridge and a cat looking like mouse,

"He's eating people," I think.

And I run away, again, but this time with money.

It wasn't three weeks later,

They found me running naked through a hotel lobby,

Running away from a hallucination of zombies,

Trying to eat me.

And that, was the moment I was taken into custody.

Days Apart

If you were a moon,

And I was a star,

Light years would appear days apart.

Asteroids have pierced your skin,

But craters with hold a slip of consciousness.

Brisk.

A moment killer first on my list,

But I imply and I insist,

That even though the light is dwindling,

I am always returning to the petty fixation of you.

It is crucial you understand,

The sun is shining for you.

The sun sets in a melancholy fashion,

No exemptions,

Just a particular ration of thought.

And this rain drops my thoughts on why we see things so differently.

This rain drops my thoughts on the extensions that portray,

The ice of mind that melts into a whisper...

Chapter Eight

Prisoner of War

"Can I have a cigarette?" I ask the man who cuffed me.

"I would, but I'm looking at all the crimes you are being investigated for,"

Says a man behind a computer in the Edmond's police store.

They make me change into some sort of poncho and lock me in a room,

Where I hear walkie talkies beeping and a muffled voice saying,

"We're gonna let it out."

And in my mind I'm freaking out,

Trying to connect the dots on the wall with my vision,

In order to trigger the locks and make it out of a government experiment.

I lie down completely still,

Thinking, "The mutant beast can't see me if I don't move,"

Eventually, a woman comes to the cell and lets me out,

"I have some questions to ask you," she says,

“Here, come sit down at this table.”

She places a voice recorder in the center of the room.

And tells me, “Before you answer any questions,

You have the right to consult a lawyer...

So... *Do you* want to answer these questions for me?

I have twenty of them.”

“I don’t see why not,” I tell her, still completely disoriented

From hallucinations and delusions,

Literally not of right enough mind to feed myself.

With the voice in my head saying,

“I am your lawyer and I demand you to not answer any of her questions!”

“I am your lawyer!’

“Hello! Hello?”

The questions seem to come from nowhere with no meaning to me,

Until she asks, “Is this your email address?” and she points at a piece of paper.

“I would like to talk to a lawyer, now.”

“How convenient,” She gets angry and places hand cuffs on me

And reads me my rights for the second time.

They began to transport me to Snohomish County Jail,

Cuffed with just jeans and a thermal shirt on,

Nothing to keep me warm,

And all the reasons to pray on.

Alongside the squad car is a military jeep with automatic rifles attached to the hood,

Pointed directly at me.

I begin to think,

"The MS13 sent me here to activate bombs placed at the peak of the mountains,

A hundred miles East."

And as I drive past these checkpoints,

I hear beeps of activated charms,

The bomb in my chest will explode,

The moment I make it into booking.

I stand and wait to be escorted into the county jail,

When I start to shiver, horrifically,

I can hear the bomb beeping inside of me,

And the guards don't understand why I am shaking so violently,

But something...

Someone...

Diffused me.

And they begin to process me.

They exchange my clothes for green pants,

No underwear, No socks,

Just a striped jumpsuit supplied by the cops.

And I can't help, but notice the different colors,

The different cells,

The fact that I spent eight hours without a meal,

Finally, they bring us cat food sandwiches,

And my throat begins to swell up,

Before they gave me liquid Benadryl,

And put me in a cell all by myself,

The Catholic I was would tell me I am in hell,

But the first lucid and waking instinct I can decipher tells me,

This is an experimental facility,

Duplicated as a jail,

Within in it are the zombie experiments,

The reason I am here,

Isn't because I deserve to be,

But because nazis control this city.

I may have been a lot of things in my life,

But I definitely wasn't no *nazi zombie*.

And before I can start panicking,

The Benadryl settles in my stomach, in this fridge, in this cell,

In this ward, I see sacred geometry spreading across the wall,

Like chocolate milk the drips of triangles slither in my heart,

And I can't help, but think, there's something wrong with this building.

Because there's something wrong with me.

And something wrong doesn't meld well with society.

So, they take the wrong, and put it with other wrongs

So, we can all be wrong together.

The only wrong part about it is how they treat the people,

Who recognize the something wrong in themselves,

And would rather be in school learning morals than stuck in 8 by 4 cells.

They photograph my standing self.

And ask me about the tattoos on my arm.

I was speaking gibberish and then never quite figured out if the cross tattooed to my left arm was a gang symbol, even though it's a hieroglyphic that has no relation to any gang.

"Do you have any illnesses we should know about," they ask,

"I am disabled from PTSD," I respond politely,

"What would you do if we released you today?" an officer asks me.

"I would kill myself."

As I am escorted into ankle and wrist cuffs,

In my green jump suit,

I politely ask the man detaining me,

"Where am I? Where am I going?"

"A place with a lot of privacy," he responds as if my life means something.

Red dots scatter across two-way mirrors,

My retina fuses with the lack of oxygen

And I feel a looming wakefulness sliding into perception,
The lack of food inhibits the digestion of this process
For wrong people,
In between wrong walls,
In the bird's nest where zombies crawl.

My heart stalls, as it is slowly sinking in,
I'm being held captive,
"For military reasons,"
I think,
"Serbia will come for me soon,
It's unlikely that a refugee will lose in court."

But my time is kept short,
Before I am uncuffed and shoved into a cell,
With nothing more than a brown paper bag,
Filled with the rules of jail;
I couldn't even read.
But this was the least of my troubles,
As time starts to lose its meaning...
I pass out thinking the cuffs are still on me.
A phantom.

Something so softly wakes me up,
Like the dry sound of pencil on paper,
Irritating to say the least,
The paper slides under the cell door and hits my feet.
The paper reads,
Four different felonies.

Save Me, MS13

There's a third eye blinded by all that are able.
You might not know this, but I am disabled.
Still.
I look to my third eye for what's real, and what's right,
When you have no need to focus,
You have no need for time,
The common plight.

Reverberating in between focal points,
I am disturbed by changing lights,
Every time I live through this thought,
A little bit of me dies inside.
I may not even be thirty,
But I think I am in my midlife.

Crisis everted.
Why do I even try?

There's a lot to be said, but more to be done.
There's a lot of wars to explain to our daughters and sons.

There are a lot of guns.

One for each of us to be exact.

Rebel armies will never have your back.

Chapter Nine

Sensory Deprivation

The light is always on.
I flick the switch,
Nothing.

The light is always on,
Depriving me of darkness,
The nothingness.

Something,
Turns in my void.
Conquered in time I try to avoid,
Flipping the switch in my brain,
Because every time I flick the switch,
Blades fall from all directions.
The invisible death.

This blanket protects me with scratches.
If I hold it over my shoulders long enough,
I begin to morph,

Into a venomous rapture.

Standing on the roof.

I begin to understand that this is the end of the end.

The decaying of all mankind,

But the KGB is going to save me.

They'll break into my cell,

Before I hear the doors open and slam beneath my cell.

"Dinner's served!" someone yells.

"I've been waiting for this meal my entire life," someone declares from two cells over.

They put me on a special diet.

Something I would eat every day:

Rice.

A beef patty, no bun,

And a side salad-I'm sure someone pissed on.

And occasionally some milk.

With it comes a butter packet, that I save,

Every day,

Until I have ten of them, and feast on butter to keep myself alive.

I heard over ten people died in this jail in the past year.
And tears don't explain the torture this place has on a brain.
Mine was already decaying.
No medication to give me the feeling that I am alive.
It goes without saying,
I cried and I...
I almost died from starvation.

Looking down at the dark side of my hand,
I think back to when I was ten,
"Hello shadow! Where have you been?"

Your loose grip reminds me of when I lived,
At Brendan's house for a night,
When we compared favorite every things.
When we tried to be friends.

"Hello Shadow! Where have you been?"
The words echo inside my head,
Back and forth,
Through torture comes words,
I would only utter if it were the end.

"I miss you Brendan,
I don't know where you are,
Or if you can hear me.
Your memories are starting to coerce me,
Into believing,
That the person I've been remembering,
Hasn't always been me."

A perfect reflection.
Only the mind can see.
And I request witness protection,
To every person that visits my cell.

Hoping the message has already been received,
Prior to this oncoming hell.

I start to remember myself,
Through his eyes.
I am only beginning to understand the lengths people will go,
To silence a witness.

Spiders.

Giant fucking spiders.

And a ghost mop.

Shackles and chains restraining a venomous murderer.

But the spiders,

Came from swamps.

And their legs could stab you through the heart,

Pick you apart,

And leave you in the swamp to die.

Someone bangs on my cell with a knife.

Solitary confinement has no eyes.

The only vision coming with an altitude of fear,

And these spiders can hear me breathing,

"You just gonna pretend to sleep?"

The spider says to me.

Sharp as nails,

I turn over in my cell.

It would have been nice to have a book,

To tear to shreds,
To diffuse the bomb in my chest.
But the sharp nails pierce my brain,
Like the shackles that restrain, Anthony.

“He’s coming for me...” I think.
Vengeance is venom is artery and vein,
I can’t remember the love I had,
For this runaway.

Computer crash my empty cash,
My hand is bleeding blue.
I fold my hands and pray as if God would hear me, too.
I see a woman,
Within a hallucination caused by sensory deprivation.
Here in this cell,
I’m breathing the words that Molly would sell me out with,
“I’m gonna bust you,” she says, years before we ever met.

A red dot, from a two-way mirror,
Reminds me to slow down, eating my extra dinner.

These are segments of time,

In a timeless trap,

Where X’s on the walls, dictate the time and path.

Looking back, at a glance, within a glimpse-of the other side,

I realize...

It’s not you,

It’s the language you speak.

It’s how you must keep yourself at the peak of each conversation.

Plain and simple, I’m getting weak,

Eating butter,

No speak.

60 pounds disappears from me.

And I am beginning to think,

These four felonies might be real.

And the cell I am in is a worm.

The mouth is the door,

I’m being absorbed by a building.

I pretend to smoke a cig,

And the invisible death grants me my wish.

Nicotine pops in my lungs,

And I finish it,

Hoping the worm won't see me.

Desperately,

I begin to break my skull.

One THUD.

Two THUD.

Three THUD, Four,

I'm bleeding from my ears and hoping this will even the score.

Because if my actions make me who I am,

And I am and was delusional,

Then I am a delusional person,

Who deserves to die.

I didn't cry,

Concussed,

I should have died.

But they escorted me to the padded room.

They made me strip and wear a velcro vest-that wouldn't stick and keep me dressed.

So, every time they wanted to talk, I had to show them my hands,

And the vest would fall,

Leaving me naked,

In between padded walls.

"He's sexually harassing me," the woman yells.

And she labels me as, "Gravely Disabled."

And fights to press charges against me,

For having my clothes taken,

Inevitably naked.

The torture of choice.

I start thinking,

"I need to walk in patterns to unlock the doors,"

So, in a crazy wave of subconsciousness,

I sporadically move in all directions,

Until, they finally give me some medication.

They gave me dinner, a real meal for once,

But didn't give me a fork to eat it with.

So, I just starred at this tray of food,

Thinking back to junior high,

Which is why I am not allowed to have food.

I think, “My dad is a cannibal.”

Eventually I made it to court,

But couldn’t even report to them with words,

I almost passed out in front of the judge when he asked me what I plead.

And two months into solitary confinement meant,

They finally motioned for me to be sent to Western State Hospital.

Where I learned the term, “Diminished Capacity.”

I Started Writing

I started writing again,
In the hospital.

I walked in with a prisoner's beard,
An empty stomach,
And a traumatic brain injury that was never addressed.

I couldn't help but feel like I had been here before...

Chapter Ten

Western State Hospital

These are my friends.

They understand that I don't always say what I mean.

They understand me.

Because we have similarities.

"Everyone here has committed a crime," a nurse says to me.

I no longer believe we are innocent until proven guilty.

This hospital was less like a hospital,

More so a penitentiary.

When you hear, "CODE BLUE," over the speakers,

You know someone almost died.

When you go outside,

Don't bring back a flower like my friend did for me.

Guns drawn,

You always come inside empty handed.

A dandelion is dangerous to an open mind.

A flower pedal,

Disintegrates in time.

They started me out in patient room 15.

Where a dotted yellow line separates me from the other patients.

I pick up a random book and start to read,

But I haven't really slept in two months,

So, the moment my head hits that pillow,

I crash.

The first task I had was to shave my beard,

Scratchy and curly, I look disgusting.

And my fingernails are stuck in the 80's.

Buzz, buzz, buzz,

I start demolishing.

Really polishing my face.

They gave me sweats and a sweater,

Much more comfortable than the cheap plastic leather in jail.

No velcro keeping my clothes on.

And room to walk around as if I had something going on.

Orange sweater.

Orange sweats.

Socks and underwear, a luxury most of us forget.

And hey, some people that could be my friends...

I ingest the first real meal I've had in two months.

And everyone lines up and leaves the ward.

While I stay and watch T.V.

These places have a nasty tendency to not tell you your responsibilities.

They let me stay upstairs for the first three days,

Eventually transferring me to patient room 2,

"Because of your progress," they said.

When really all I did was take the random medication they gave me,

Without ever telling me what it is.

I started talking with other patients,

The fact that I finished my food resumes in the nurse's head,

"He must be faking," I'm sure she is thinking.

I see another patient admitted into the ward,

I scream at the top of my head, “FIRE SCANDEL!”

A threat no one understood.

His name...?

For the sake of revolution,

He was my long lost and fraternal twin flame,

Who would walk with me every day,

And talk about the reasons we came to the hospital.

“I think they gave me Zannex first,

And then Klonopin,

I told them I don’t want any addictive medications,”

And my twin flame insisted, “Man, that’s the good shit, why are you telling them you don’t want it?”

“Because I want to be healthy,” I explain to him.

I made another friend in the hospital.

I didn’t realize he was serious,

But he started mapping out a plan for the two of us.

We would escape the hospital and take a loan from a mob,

Then buy drugs, sell them, and vacation on an island for multiple weeks,

Until we needed to pay the mob back,

Then we would take a loan from another mob to pay that mob,

And continue the cycle for the rest of our lives.

I honestly thought it was just fun and games, until they started questioning me about my potential escape.

However, I didn't really feel like going anywhere.

I mean, I thought two of the patients were wearing someone else's skin,

I also thought I was in the Secret Service here to investigate a jail and hospital.

Nothing really made sense to me at this place,

But for some reason I had a great time.

Compared to jail, the hospital is a vacation.

Here I learned in class that you can plead diminished capacity and if proven,

Your case would be dismissed or lowered to a misdemeanor.

I asked, "What is *Diminished Capacity*?"

The teacher responded, "When you have no intent to commit a crime, but the actions are yours."

Looking back, at a glance,

Within a glimpse of the other side,

I realize...

Brendan died on April 19th, 2009 at the age 16 and a half.

And the next day, 4/20/2009 was the day my cat, Bella, was born.

This is the day I started to believe in reincarnation.

Eventually,

Through all the private encounters and endeavors that happen in a hospital,

They decided to give me an I.Q. test,

To see where I was at.

The doctor says he is going to ask me a series of questions,

I need to respond immediately with the first thought that comes to mind,

And he eventually asks me a question in the form of a metaphor,

And I respond with another metaphor.

He said, “Well, you are very intelligent, but I can’t tell you how intelligent, because you didn’t answer the last question.”

They decided to end my 30 day minimum stay at Western State Hospital at day 25.

Determining that my capacity has been restored.

I returned to the jail and they immediately put me back in solitary confinement,

For about 5 hours,

Until they realized they were being fined thousands of dollars for every day I spent in solitary confinement,

Part of a class action lawsuit I would receive 40 dollars for.

So, they transferred me to a section of the jail for people with my type of offense.

And this is where I made some real friends.

At one point I got half the people in the ward to recite the words to the song, “Because I got high,”

And they looked the other way as I practiced Tai Chi in the outside room,

Martial arts were forbidden.

I had bought about ten candy bars with the money on my books,

And the last night I was in jail,

I had a party with my cell mate.

At one point the guard banged on our doors and had to remind us that we were in jail...

Fuck that guy.

A Story with no End

Brendan was probably the most beloved person I have ever met,

He was legally dead for about five minutes before the gym teacher resuscitated him.

That's a long time for the brain to be deprived of oxygen.

And the day it happened every child in the fifth grade cried through their lunch.

We were all sent home early.

Brendan spent over a year in Children Hospital's ICU,

And I tried to visit him there, but it was limited to direct family.

Until one day I went to the hospital and asked if he was there,

The nurse said he was sent home, and began to cry.

"Do you know him?" she asked.

"Yes."

About six years later after partially learning how to talk again,

After seeing a movie with me and talking on the phone for countless hours,

Brendan was on the road to recovery,

But unfortunately, he suffered cardiac arrest once again while in treatment in Arizona.

With all of his family and friends in mind,

Brendan died peacefully in his sleep on April 19th, 2009.

I never got to ask him out on a date.

Chapter Eleven

Saying Goodbye

I was released from jail on April 18th, 2014

After spending two months in solitary confinement and one month in the hospital.

With the known disorder of Chronic PTSD and the eventual diagnosis of Schizo Affective Disorder; Depressive Type,

I had to piece back together my life.

I was arrested for an inappropriate email I sent when I was so delusional, I thought my dad was eating people and that zombies controlled the city of Seattle.

I plead guilty under diminished capacity, meaning I had no intent to commit a crime.

And this was accepted as truth.

The day after I was released from jail,

About one month into my medication regiment,

I went to the graveyard one last time,

To say goodbye to, Brendan.

"Hey, Brendan," I look down at his tombstone.

Showered in gifts.

“Remind yourself,

No matter how far you take your education,

You will always need to get your pills from someone else.

Well...

Substance abuse froze and refused to save me from,

The street side performances that induce and endorphin’s run.

On the side of streets near vacant guns,

We speak of words like thunder struts.

Fun to think it is food for thought,

But when you are stuck between, atoms rot,

And all our thoughts have taken a lot out of us.

So, we ingest the concept of being healthy,

Like our pets,

Well...

At least, I hope.

Even though there’s more to life than being a serotonin drone.

Maybe our pets would want us to stop using.

Or maybe just come home.

And I know it may seem cold to say just what I see,
But when I think twice, and then I, then I speak,
Is when we appear to be,
Merely sequenced to the themes that stream through your,
Beautiful blue carbon eyes...

On second thought, I thought twice.

I mean,
I know that I know nothing.
I know not what I see, but I tend to believe in a lot of things.
And all I can see is dead flowers,
The absence of wind,
The viewpoint making its way back to my vision,
Striking my pupil and into my lens,
Through the retina and into the optic nerve,
Back to my Occipital Lobe,
With pigments fading as gases dissolve,
The image of you will be nothing at all,

Because the momentum of memory is something to solve.

Time and time again,

I see reflections of this frozen mirror image,

Let's retrace our steps to see what it takes to make angels reflect,

That we are one in the same.

Blessed rose peddle dreams,

In sync with an avenue of freedom,

In search of a perfect reflection,

In this dream I can see myself parallel with hell,

I can justify the love we sell,

I'm at an apex and I have to ask,

Is that you I see through the looking glass?

But alas, you are no more,

Forbidden words like scars from thorns,

I'll never forget the year you were born,

Or the day you passed,

FORGIVE ME, but

Dead flowers never last."

www.ingramcontent.com/pod-product-compliance
Ingram Content Group UK Ltd.
Pitfield, Milton Keynes, MK11 3LW, UK
UKHW041643190726
13854UKWH00006B/2674

9 781794 808089